Praise for Sarah Wright's

10 THINGS I WISH I KNEW ABOUT DEPRESSION

"Wow! What a wonderful piece of work! This book teaches extremely well from a place of love and experience. As a therapist, I can use this book as a tool to support clients as they explore their diagnosis of depression and experience recovery."

— *Sala I. Hilaire, LCSW, MAC, CAMS*

"Dr. Wright's clarity and guidance on the topic of depression is stellar. This step by step guide provides companionship, inspiration, and hard data to illuminate the path from recognition to relief. Science and wisdom combine beautifully here in the bright and courageous voice of Dr.

Wright. She models resilience and faith as she educates and points the way to real, practical help."

— *Kathy Malcolm Hall, MS*
Licensed Professional Counselor
Certified Imago Therapist

"Beth-Sarah Wright rightly understands that seeking professional help for depression is consistent with belief in God, faith and prayer. This book calls us all to seek healing in all its wonderful forms."

— *The Rt. Rev. Rob Wright, D.D.*
Bishop, Episcopal Diocese of Atlanta

ABOUT THE AUTHOR

Beth-Sarah Wright, PhD is an author, inspirational speaker and retreat leader on spirituality and healing. She is the author of *Me? Depressed?: A Story of Depression from Denial to Discovery* (2013) and a novel, *Weeping May Endure for a Night* (2014). She was featured in Esperanza Magazine for Anxiety and Depression as an "Everyday Hero" (2011).

Originally from Jamaica, she has lived and studied internationally, from Edinburgh, Scotland to San Juan, Puerto Rico and currently lives in Atlanta, Georgia. She earned her BA in Sociology and African-American Studies at Princeton University, her Master's in Social Anthropology at Cambridge University, and completed her doctorate in Performance Studies at New York University. She is married to Robert Wright, Episcopal Bishop of Atlanta, and mother to their five wonderful children.

Peggy,

10 THINGS I WISH I KNEW ABOUT
DEPRESSION

Before it Almost Took My Life

Thank you
for all you
do.

10 THINGS I WISH I KNEW ABOUT
DEPRESSION

Before it **Almost** *Took My Life*

A Pocket Guide to Recognize,
Respond to and Relieve Depression

Breaking Down Stigmas.
Building Hope.

Beth-Sarah Wright, PhD

All rights reserved, no part of this publication may be reproduced by any means, electronic, mechanical photocopying, documentary, film or in any other format without prior written permission of the publisher.

Copyright © 2014
Beth-Sarah Wright

Gye Nyame Publishing
3225 Beechwood Drive, SE
Marietta, GA 30067

www.bethsarahwright.com
ISBN: 978-1-304-91403-3
Printed in
The United States of America
March 2014
First Edition

Book design by
Kelly King Works, Inc.
www.kellykingworks.com

To all those who are battling depression
and to all those who love them:
Remember, there is **ALWAYS** hope!

Be joyful in hope,
patient in affliction,
faithful in prayer.
Romans 12:12

West African Adinkra symbol for Hope

CONTENTS

"Me? Depressed?" That was the question I asked the psychiatrist sitting across from me who just diagnosed me with depression about 8 years ago. It is the same question I entitled my memoir about my journey with depression, "A Story of Depression from Denial to Discovery", because I certainly was in complete denial at first! I was so blinded by the stigma and associative feelings of shame and embarrassment that come along with being "depressed," I couldn't see the gift the psychiatrist was giving me. The gift of a diagnosis. It took me another 2 years, a 2nd and 3rd opinion and a near suicide attempt to finally "get it." Oh, how I wish I knew then what I know now!

The stigma that surrounds depression is a powerful thing. When I first heard the possibility I might be depressed, I didn't get help. I didn't even accept the possibility. Instead I tried to find every excuse for it not to be true. There is no history of depression or mental illness in my immediate family. I grew up in a wonderful, stable, middle-class Christian family, and therefore, I naively assumed I was not a candidate for depression. I had achieved educationally what about 1% of the world has, and I was happily married to a wonderful man and together raising pretty awesome children. I had no alcoholism, no abuse, and no traumatic event. Nothing that, in my mind, at least would lead to depression. But I was and unnecessarily suffering for too long before ultimately recognizing and responding to what was really happening to me.

But that is the power of stigma isn't it? The power to completely distract you from seeing what is truly real. And that is a problem! Especially when your health, your life, and the lives of others can be significantly impacted. That is why I wrote this book, to try to obliterate the power of stigma, so that those who may be battling depression, and those who love them, can recognize, respond to and get relief from this illness.

How I wish that when I was first faced with the possibility of being depressed, that I had at my fingertips information (not the medical details about depression; I wasn't even ready for that!) but information that could specifically separate the cloud of stigma in my head from the reality I was feeling and experiencing! This is what I hope to provide in writing this small, pocket-sized guide book: succinct, clear, accessible and helpful information that will help to break down many of the common myths and assumptions about depression. But not only that, but to build hope and point to some resources to get help.

This book represents the "top ten" most valuable lessons I have discovered about depression since my illness began affecting my life. I first gathered them for my blog following an illuminating segment on the "Stigma of Mental Illness" on the program 60 Minutes (September 29, 2013). I was so disturbed by the pervasive misunderstanding or stigma of mental illnesses, and consequent lack of support for those impacted by them and trepidation in seeking help. The following day, I learned of the collaborative efforts by the Depression and Bipolar Support Alliance (DBSA) and the International Bipolar Foundation (IBPF) to promote Say It Forward 2013 (September 30 - October 10, 2013), "an email and social media anti-stigma campaign that educates people about the reality of mental health conditions." I used that opportunity to "say it forward" in my own way and shatter the silence around stigma, on my blog. This book is the result.

Please know that I am not a psychologist or psychiatrist. I have no official training in psychology but I do have my story, my experience. And telling my story, telling our stories is one important part of breaking down the stigmas and building up hope. This is not dispensing medical advice. I encourage you to seek more specific information from your medical doctors, psychiatrists, therapists or counselors. All the medical information and statistics used in this book to support my experiences have been taken from public information given by The World Health Organization (WHO, www.who.int), the National Alliance on Mental Illness (NAMI, www.nami.org), Refugee Health Technical Assistance Center (www.refugeehealthta.org) and the National Institute of Mental Health (NIMH, www.nimh.nih.gov). Please visit these websites for more information. The information in this book is not exhaustive. I encourage you to gather your own information from websites and health providers and counselors if you have further questions.

This book is about breaking down some common stigmas, which are really obstacles, I too believed and continue to encounter as I interact with others, that prevented me and so many from feeling comfortable and safe enough to get the help we so desperately need. Perhaps some of these stigmas have prevented you or someone you love from getting the help you or they need. I hope that these 10 discoveries will widen the understanding and conversation about depression.

My faith life has deepened tremendously over the course of my healing and has become not only the core of my self-care and mental healing, but is where the well of my hope exists.

I could not write this book without including this fundamental part of my healing. Each chapter begins with a piece of scripture, which has been instrumental in my spiritual growth and maturity and healing. I invite you to also gain strength and courage and hope from them. I can say that I am truly grateful to God for this experience of depression. It has not been easy but the discovery of joy and laughter again on this journey to wholeness and healing has truly been redemptive!

If you or someone you love is experiencing depression I pray for that taste of joy in life again.

Remember there is always hope!

CHAPTER 1

It's NOT Your Fault!

Having depression is not a choice. It is an illness, not unlike having cancer or diabetes. You did nothing to bring this on yourself. How you recognize, respond to and get relief from it, is however your choice.

Depression is an illness. Help is available. Seek it. Choose to get the help you need.

It's NOT your fault!

Create in me a clean heart, O God, and renew a right spirit within me. Cast me not away from your presence, and take not your Holy Spirit from me. Restore to me the joy of your salvation, and uphold me with a willing spirit.

Psalm 51

I WISH I KNEW...

That I did not bring this on myself nor did I choose to feel this way, nor was I less of a person for feeling this emotional pain.

When I first started experiencing what I have now come to understand as symptoms of depression- the complete lack of interest in anything I used to enjoy, the extreme self-doubt and low self-esteem, the self-loathing, the feelings of worthlessness—I assumed it was my fault: "I am just too lazy", "I am not trying hard enough", "I am not smart enough", "I am not being Christian enough", "What am I doing wrong?" and "I am a failure." See the pattern?

My thinking was I that I was bringing this on myself, and if only I fixed those things, moved to the land of "enough", I would feel better. This is like saying, I have just been diagnosed with breast cancer and it is my fault. I caused this. Ludicrous!

Recently, a man said to me after reading the title of my book, "Oh, I am too busy to be depressed." As if keeping busy can stave off this illness. I was stunned and wished I had some smart and witty retort for him but I did not. It reminded me however, that this type of thinking, this type of misinformation is prevalent and prevents those who may be battling depression to feel comfortable and safe to get the necessary help.

The most pivotal moment in my healing journey was when I recognized that I am a woman battling depression, not a depressed woman. It is not my fault. I did not bring this on myself. But I can get help!

SOME FACTS TO DE-"STIGMA"-TIZE:

- Depression is a chronic illness, a serious emotional and biological disease. It affects one's thoughts, feelings, behavior, mood and physical health.

- An estimated 25 million American adults are affected by major depression in a given year.

- Globally, more than 350 million people of all ages are affected by depression.

- Depression is the leading cause of disability worldwide.

- Depression can be treated!

Adapted from public information from The World Health Organization (WHO, www.who.int), the National Alliance on Mental Illness (NAMI, www.nami.org), Refugee Health Technical Assistance Center (www.refugeehealthta.org) and the National Institute of Mental Health (NIMH, www.nimh.nih.gov).

CHAPTER 2

It's NOT Just the Blues!

We all feel sad for some reason or other at many times in our lives. But having depression is something fundamentally different and may affect your daily life for weeks at a time, sometimes years. This is not something you can "shake off" or "pray away" (although prayer is great!) or "get over". It's nothing to be ashamed of or embarrassed about. It is not a sign of being "weak".

Relief is possible!

For I will restore health to you,
and your wounds I will heal,
declares the Lord.
Jeremiah 30

I WISH I KNEW...

My persistent sadness was a sign of something more serious, an illness and that I needed help.

My depression manifested in severe sadness and lack of energy and interest in many aspects of my life. I couldn't wait to lie back in bed after taking the kids to school and I had no interest in cooking, for myself or others, or cleaning; my work became a burden, it was so difficult to concentrate and focus and I wanted to call in sick many a day.

I kept thinking however, other folks also have kids and work and they just seem to snap out of their sadness or fatigue. Why can't I? Why am I different? Why won't it go away? Maybe a vacation will do it, or a change in pace.

Maybe I should pray more. So many people have it harder than I do, why can't I just be normal and be happy with who I am and what I have?

I never thought about going to a doctor or getting treatment in any way. When I fully realized that depression is a physiological and emotional illness, that is, my feelings were intimately tied to my flesh and blood, my brain chemistry, I finally decided to see a psychiatrist and get the help I needed. It was the beginning to a journey of healing and discovery!

SOME FACTS TO DE- "STIGMA"-TIZE:

- Depression may occur spontaneously with no observable trigger and may be unassociated with any life crisis, physical illness or other currently known risks.

- Depression may occur as a result of multiple factors: A person's life, experience, genetic inheritance, substance abuse and other illnesses.

- Depression may be "unipolar" or "bipolar". *Unipolar*: typically the person experiences depressed mood, loss of interest and enjoyment, reduced energy for at least two weeks. May be mild, moderate or severe. *Bipolar*: usually consists of both manic and depressive episodes separated by periods of normal mood. Manic episodes involve elevated or irritable mood, over-activity, pressure of speech, inflated self-esteem and a decreased need for sleep. (They have different treatments. Accurate diagnosis is crucial)

- Other types of depression include Dysthymia (persistent depressive disorder for more than two years), Seasonal

Affective disorder (SAD) (usually strikes in fall and winter), Melancholic depression (Loss of pleasure in about all activities), Atypical depression (depression with temporary mood elevation), Psychotic (includes delusions or hallucinations) and Catatonic (marked by excessive involuntary physical movement or inactivity as if patient is paralyzed).

See Dr. Sanjay Gupta, Everyday Health (www.everydayhealth.com).

- Although there are known, effective treatments for depression, fewer than half of those affected in the world receive such treatments due to: a lack of resources, lack of trained health care providers, lack of bilingual health care providers, cultural barriers, and social stigma associated with mental disorders.

- Culture biases against mental health professionals and health care professionals in general prevent many African Americans from accessing care due to prior experiences with historical misdiagnoses, inadequate treatment and a lack of cultural understanding; only 2% of psychiatrists, 2% of psychologists and 4% of social workers in the United States are African American.

- Fewer than 1 in 20 Latino immigrants use services from mental health specialists.

COMMON SYMPTOMS OF DEPRESSION:

- Feeling sad or empty;

- Loss of interest in favorite activities

- Low self-esteem; Feeling, irritable, anxious, or guilty. During periods of depression, people dwell on memories of losses or failures (sometimes perceived) and feel excessive helplessness.

- Feelings of hopelessness or guilt. The symptoms of depression often produce a strong feeling of hopelessness, or a belief that nothing will ever improve. These feelings can lead to thoughts of suicide.

- Feeling very tired; loss of energy. Mental speed and activity are usually reduced, as is the ability to perform normal daily routines.

- Poor concentration. The inability to concentrate and/or make decisions is a serious aspect of depression. During severe depression, some people find following the thread of a simple newspaper article to be extremely difficult, or making major decisions often impossible.

- Not being able to sleep, or sleeping too much.

- Changes in appetite: Overeating, or not wanting to eat at all; weight gain or weight loss.

- Movement changes. People may literally look "slowed down" or overly activated and agitated.

- Thoughts of suicide, suicide attempts

- Persistent physical symptoms that do not respond to treatment, such as headaches, digestive disorders and chronic pain

Sometimes depression manifests itself differently from group to group and may not be recognized as depression and therefore may go untreated.

Some examples:

MEN AND DEPRESSION

Men in particular do not usually display observable symptoms. While not well understood, men are less likely to show "typical" signs of depression such as crying, sadness, loss of interest in previously enjoyable activities or verbally expressing thoughts of suicide. Depression may actually cause men to suppress their feelings and become more aggressive or irritable. Men may try to "tough it out" or sometimes self-medicate using alcohol or drugs or engage in risky behavior. Because of this health providers and others may not recognize the illness.

DEPRESSION IN OLDER PERSONS

Depression in older persons often go untreated because many people think it is a normal part of aging, or may attribute the depressive symptoms as signs of other disorders like dementia, Alzheimer's disease, arthritis, cancer, heart disease, Parkinson's disease, stroke or thyroid disorders.

Symptoms in older persons are at times characterized by: memory problems, confusion, social withdrawal, loss of appetite, weight loss, vague complaints of pain, inability to sleep, irritability, delusions (fixed false beliefs) and hallucinations.

Adapted from public information from The World Health Organization (WHO, www.who.int), the National Alliance on Mental Illness (NAMI, www.nami.org), Refugee Health Technical Assistance Center (www.refugeehealthta.org) and the National Institute of Mental Health (NIMH, www.nimh.nih.gov).

CHAPTER 3

Depression Does NOT Discriminate

You don't have to be a certain age or race or gender, or come from a certain background, or from a certain culture to have depression. Depression can affect you regardless of how much money you have or don't have or how much education you have achieved or not. Many might ask "Why me?" but the question might more accurately be "Why not you?"

Depression does NOT discriminate!

God gives his best—the sun to warm
and the rain to nourish—to everyone, regardless.
Matthew 5

I WISH I KNEW…

**That being educated or coming from a
stable loving home, did not exclude me from
having depression.**

Having depression is not a "white" thing, a
"rich" thing, a "poor" thing, a "homeless" thing
or a "woman" thing. Depression does not
necessarily affect one population more than
another. I confess, I thought that having
depression was relegated to
"artists/poets/writers" almost as a prerequisite
to being talented. I thought having a mental
illness, meant you were on the street,
"homeless", barefoot and talking to yourself; I
thought depression was for very wealthy folks
who had the "luxury" of having a mental illness;

I thought being depressed was more for women than men.

It wasn't until I was admitted to a mental health hospital to receive treatment that I saw in real time the pervasiveness of depression. There I met men and women; old and young; doctors, lawyers, nurses, bankers; Asian, Black, White, Latino; purple, pink and green folk ALL suffering with depression or some sort of a mental illness. I realized as I sat in group therapy with them and we shared our stories that it did not matter where or how you grew up, how much you money you had or didn't have; if you were religious or not; it is an illness, and it does NOT discriminate.

One very common assumption is that depression affects women more than men. But the jury is still out on that. It may be that women have more hormone imbalances than men do, which may affect brain chemistry more. But it may be that women are more inclined to admit needing help and seek it more readily than men. Regardless, men and women alike experience depression, and it is not something to be ashamed of.

As a Jamaican and an anthropologist, I am also sensitive to the cross-cultural understandings of depression. Some people believe that depression is an "American" thing. A woman once asked, "Did Americans make up post-partum depression, because you rarely if ever hear about it in other countries?"

The facts don't lie. Depression is a global phenomenon. It may be approached and addressed in different ways, for example the word depression does not exist in certain Asian languages, but that does not mean it does not exist. Depression may even occur at different rates due to environmental contexts, or people may not seek treatment due to cultural beliefs and practices.

Depression can affect anyone regardless of these differences. And similarly, depression may also be understood and approached differently across cultural groups within the United States. For example, Latinos are twice as likely to seek treatment for mental disorders in other settings, such as the clergy, than in mental health specialty settings due to cultural understandings about depression. The facts remain however. Depression is real. It occurs globally. It is an illness and does not discriminate!

SOME FACTS TO DE- "STIGMA"-TIZE:

- Depression affects more than 6.5 million of the 35 million Americans aged 65 or older.

- On any single day in America, about 2% of school-aged children and about 8% of adolescents meet the criteria for major depression. 1 in 5 teens have had a history of depression.

- Experiences of mental illness vary across cultures, and there is a need for improved cultural awareness and competence in the health care and mental health workforce.

- Depression in Latino communities: Prevalence of depression is higher in Latina women (46%) than Latino men (19.6%)

- Latinas don't want to be viewed as "*loca*" because of the stigma attached to it.

- Depression is the second leading cause of death in Asian and Pacific Islander Americans.

- Approximately 20% of youth ages 13 to 18 experience severe mental disorders in a given year.

- Approximately 60% of adults and almost 1/2 of youth ages 8 to 15 with a mental illness received no mental health services in the previous year.

- African-American and Hispanic Americans used mental health services at about 1/2 the rate of Caucasians in the past year and Asian Americans at about 1/3 the rate.

- Veterans account for slightly more than 14% of the total population of persons diagnosed with depression.

Adapted from public information from The World Health Organization (WHO, www.who.int), the National Alliance on Mental Illness (NAMI, www.nami.org), Refugee Health Technical Assistance Center (www.refugeehealthta.org) and the National Institute of Mental Health (NIMH, www.nimh.nih.gov).

CHAPTER 4

There is No "One Size Fits All" Depression!

Not all forms of depression are the same. There is no ONE reason for being depressed or ONE way to be depressed. Depression does not always look the same way. But it makes no sense to compare our experiences to others. Depression is depression, no matter what it looks like. Rather, we can better help ourselves by sharing our stories and getting the treatment we need.

Depression is not the same for everyone

Remember your word to your servant in which you have made me hope. This is my comfort in my affliction, that your promise gives me life. .
Psalm 119

I WISH I KNEW...

That depression could look differently and be caused by different reasons from person to person. Nonetheless depression is real, no matter.

I know when I was first diagnosed with depression I was in complete denial. Denial because of the stigma I attached to it, denial because I could not pinpoint any one event or crisis that I could say, "that made me depressed." I assumed I had to have endured something traumatic. But I had experienced nothing of the sort and therefore thought I was just in a funk and it would pass soon. It was that kind of un-informed thinking that prevented me from getting the treatment I needed at that time.

My first chapter in my book "Me? Depressed?" is "Aren't You Going to Take My Blood?" I wanted physical proof of this illness. I wanted the doctor to show me without a doubt why I was not well and why I had to take medication to help. I still cannot tell you why I had that episode of major depression. It could have been that my family life, 5 children, marriage, and my work overwhelmed me. It could have been that that my hormones were in flux having had babies. It could have been my extremely low self-esteem and negative self-talk which was pervasive. It could be that I received some genetic predisposition from a recessive gene somewhere in my family. I don't know. But I needed help.

I know it doesn't make sense to compare my depression to others. "I'm not as depressed as she is…" therefore I must disregard what I'm feeling. Cancer is cancer. Diabetes is diabetes. Depression is depression.

I now know what it feels like and that I don't want to be there again. I know what my triggers are. I understand better self-care. I understand loving myself. Looking back, I wish I had a more comprehensive understanding of the possible causes of depression. Perhaps I would not have chosen denial and I would've sought help sooner.

"There is no single cause of major depression. Psychological, biological and environmental factors, that is, life experience, age, sex, genetic inheritance, brain chemistry imbalance, hormone changes, substance abuse and other illnesses, may all contribute to its development. Scientific research has firmly established that major depression is a biological, medical illness. There is also an increased risk for developing depression when there is a family history of the illness." (National Alliance on Mental Illness, www.nami.com).

Some Possible Factors that Trigger Depression:

SITUATIONAL/ENVIRONMENTAL:

- Depression may be triggered by life events-loss of a loved one, loss of a job; while getting a divorce, being completely overwhelmed, post-retirement, significant transitional events, facing medical vulnerability and mortality in older persons; traumatic experiences.

- LGBTQ people may be at higher risk for depression due to societal stigma and resulting prejudice and discrimination that they may face on a regular basis from society at large, but also from family members, peers, co-workers and classmates.

- Cultural expectations in a particular community may put some persons at risk, for example, in some traditional cultures, females are supposed to be "perfect" daughters, wives, mothers and nurturers, always putting others before themselves.

- According to NAMI, persons who immigrated recently to the United States and have to adjust to a new culture are more likely to have major depression than others. Lack of acculturation, or adjustment to the new culture, may lead to problems because of issues like self-esteem and stress.

- A study found conclusively that in the Latino community, long-term residence in the United States significantly increased rates in mental disorders, with particularly dramatic increases in the rates of substance abuse.

- Refugees are at risk: rates of depression in adults (5-15%) in children: (6-40%), due to factors including number of traumas, delayed asylum application process, detention, and the loss of culture and support systems.

- Veterans are at risk: younger US veterans with depression are at the most risk for suicide (95%), middle-aged (75%) and elderly (90%); Veterans struggling with their diagnoses were more likely to commit suicide or battle with substance abuse.

Some symptoms may be short-term, but others may last for much longer. If they do, seek help.

GENETIC PRE-DISPOSITION

Some persons are genetically predisposed to depression, like some folks are more susceptible to diabetes or high blood pressure.

OTHER PHYSIOLOGICAL ISSUES:

- Menopause

- Post-partum (approximately 15% of women experience post-partum depression)

- There is a link between depression and those who have celiac disease or non-celiac gluten sensitivity.

- Having thyroid disease can also affect your mood significantly.

Adapted from public information from The World Health Organization (WHO, www.who.int), the National Alliance on Mental Illness (NAMI, www.nami.org), Refugee Health Technical Assistance Center (www.refugeehealthta.org) and the National Institute of Mental Health (NIMH, www.nimh.nih.gov).

CHAPTER 5

Depression Can Hurt... Physically

Did you know that depression can hurt? I'm not talking about emotional pain. I'm talking about physical pain! Like vague aches and pains, perhaps even chronic pain. I was surprised to find out that being depressed could actually lead to physical pain in my body.

Depression can actually hurt!

For I consider that the sufferings
of this present time are not worth
comparing with the glory
that is to be revealed to us.
Romans 8

I WISH I KNEW...

That the mysterious aches and pains I was having were associated with depression and I could have asked my doctor about it.

When I finally accepted that I had a mental illness, and it was highly recommended to take medication to feel better, I felt I had a good grasp on things. But when after taking medication for a while and I began to feel better emotionally, I found I still did not feel better physically. I was still experiencing mysterious persistent back pains and stomach issues that were just not helping matters. But then my psychiatrist informed me of the correlation between emotional dis-ease and physical symptoms. They were connected!

My psychiatrist and I worked on experimenting with different medications to tackle the physical as well as emotional symptoms.

I share this to say that sometimes there is more to this depression than previously understood. Sometimes mysterious pains may indicate emotional dis-ease and you may need to look into it. Also vice versa. When I shared this on my blog, someone wrote back, "This is so true. I have sore joints all the time. Always have." And another shared that "the pain can go beyond soreness and mild discomfort. I frequently get sharp chest pains where I am unable to move because it hurts so badly." It occurs more often than we think.

SOME FACTS TO DE- "STIGMA"-TIZE:

According to Dr. Daniel K. Hall-Flavin of the Mayo Clinic, "Pain and depression are closely related. Depression can cause pain — and pain can cause depression. Sometimes pain and depression create a vicious cycle in which pain worsens symptoms of depression, and then the resulting depression worsens feelings of pain. In many people, depression causes unexplained physical symptoms such as back pain or headaches. This kind of pain may be the first or the only sign of depression." (www.mayoclinic.org).

One disorder that has been shown to occur with depression is fibromyalgia (National Institute of Mental Health).

SOME PHYSICAL SYMPTOMS ASSOCIATED WITH DEPRESSION:

- Chronic pain, headaches, muscle aches and joint pains.

- Other physical symptoms may include: back pain, chest pain, digestive problems, dizziness or lightheadedness, exhaustion and fatigue, sleep (either too much or too little) or a change in appetite or weight.

- The manifestation of physical illnesses related to mental health, otherwise known as somatization occurs at a rate of 15% among African Americans and 9% among Caucasian Americans.

Adapted from public information from The World Health Organization (WHO, www.who.int), the National Alliance on Mental Illness (NAMI, www.nami.org), Refugee Health Technical Assistance Center (www.refugeehealthta.org) and the National Institute of Mental Health (NIMH, www.nimh.nih.gov).

CHAPTER 6

Having Willpower or Prayer is Great But NOT Enough!

Ever think "I can get through this by sheer willpower or by praying harder"? I certainly did! But while very helpful, perhaps even necessary, neither are enough. Having a mental illness is a physiological condition that needs treatment. It may require medicine, in addition to other forms of treatment to address it.

It does not make you "weak" if you need medicine or therapy to get relief.

I can do all things through him who strengthens me.
Philippians 4

I WISH I KNEW...

That taking medication to feel better emotionally was not a bad thing and did not make me a weak person.

"I'm not a strong enough Christian!", "I'm not praying enough!", "I'm not strong enough to take care of this on my own." These are all sorts of thoughts that ran rampant in my head when I was first told that I would need medication to "feel" better. It just didn't make sense to me. I also heard similar sentiments to these when I was in the hospital getting treatment. I learned that there were so many people who refused to take medication because it made them feel weak.

Thinking that willpower or prayer is enough is like *negotiating* with a hemorrhaging wound to stop the bleeding. It's just not enough!

As a lifelong Christian, I believe in the power of prayer and the role it plays in my healing and strengthening. I also know that in the deepest part of my depression I couldn't pray. I also know that when I could not, others were praying for me. I know that the answer to prayer can be "seek professional help." I believe that God placed the passion and gift of healing in individuals who have been trained and who have the expertise to help and to create medicine that can also help. I do not believe it is against God to seek medical treatment and it is not a sign of weakness to seek help either.

In "Me? Depressed?" I offered my "7 P's of Medication". Below are quotes from my memoir summarizing each, and one additional

"P" just for this book. As you heal some, more than others, may take precedence or may even be eliminated altogether. But together, they all play a significant role in healing from and relieving depression.

PRESCRIPTION MEDICINE:

"It is imperative to keep taking the medicine (even when you begin to feel great) to give it time, to give it a chance to work with your body. After all it may not be the right fit."

Anti-depressants and other prescription medicine are crucial when addressing a biological illness as depression. Depending on your specific situation, taking medicine may be a lifelong activity, and for others, it may be a temporary one. (After 3 years of medication I was able to wean off and manage my illness with other self-care strategies). Other treatments may include: Bright light therapy, acupuncture, nutritional supplements, electroconvulsive therapy, meditation, hypnosis, massage therapy, and others are being created especially for those persons who are resistant to more traditional methods.

PSYCHOTHERAPY:

"I see psychotherapy as an opportunity to talk in a safe environment with someone whose professional expertise guarantees confidentiality. It is a time to be unafraid because this person hopefully has your healing in interest and wants to help".

Psychotherapy is defined as the treatment of mental disorders by counseling and psychoanalysis. There are several types of psychotherapy shown to be effective for depression including cognitive-behavioral therapy (CBT) and interpersonal therapy (IPT). Mild to moderate depression can often be treated successfully with either of these therapies alone. More severe appears more likely to respond to a combination of psychotherapy and medication. You don't have to see a psychiatrist to get this help. "Seeing a shrink" is often itself such a stigma. Professional counselors, psychologists and therapists also do psychotherapy. And it is OK to see one. After all, would you go to a gynecologist if you had a toothache?

POSITIVE SELF-THINKING:

"For me, psychotherapy is about learning to change my behavior which in truth are destructive. My most challenging behavioral change has been to adopt positive self-thought, that is making the choice to say something positive to myself rather than my more familiar tearing down myself."

Positive self-thinking is fundamental to my present self-care strategies. When I realized I said more damaging things to myself, more than anyone ever did in my life, I knew that had to change. It took working with a therapist over years to realize that and to systematically adopt new behavior. Consider your thoughts, what you say to yourself. Are they helpful? Do you need to change? Be kind to yourself. Love yourself. Forgive yourself. You are enough!

PSYCHIATRISTS:

"Psychiatrists must be a part of your healing if you are on medication. They are the ones who know what to prescribe, how much and what interacts well or not so well with what. Sometimes a particular drug may not work and others need to be tried, and it is the psychiatrist who manages the medication. Psychologists, professional therapists etc. cannot."

Find one who works well with you and who you can work well with.

PRAYER:

"I did not get angry with God, but... I could find no peace, no answer, and no consolation in prayer and so like my medicine, I stopped praying. But it was in this time of silence that I heard, like a scream torpedoing through the air, an elixir through the scripture, 'In the same way the Spirit also comes to help us, weak as we are, when we do not know what to pray, the Spirit pleads with God for us in groans that words cannot express' (*Romans 8:26*)."

My faith life is integral to my healing. I am so grateful to God for the healing in my depression; thankful for providing folks who pointed me to seek professional help; for working through those who have this expertise. I am thankful for God's story and Jesus' story showing me what courage and faith and hope and love looks like in the face of suffering. Thankful for the stories that laughter will wipe away tears; that light will shatter the darkness; that new life comes from lifeless bodies, that death is not the end, only a new beginning; that there is always hope, and that when you choose to walk with God, the fruits of the Spirit are "love, joy, peace, patience, kindness, goodness, faithfulness, gentleness and self-control." So pray. Lean on your faith life. Weave your story into your faith story.

PEOPLE:

"As a woman I met in the hospital said to me with such insight, "community takes the "c" out of crazy."

Knowing that others have experienced depression makes you feel less "crazy", less alone and less different. I found it liberating. Freedom. Mental emancipation! Share your story, with those who you feel worthy and can trust. Seek out a support group, share with family and friends. Dare to be vulnerable. Denial and shame thrives in silence. Choose not to be silent. Also give of yourself, your time and talent to other people. Volunteering, stepping outside of yourself may also significantly impact the way you feel and see the world. Don't keep it to yourself. Don't be silent. Share your story. Empower yourself and others by embracing your story.

PLAYING:

"*I heard a psychiatrist say that for thirty years he has been prescribing a medication that his patients continually refuse to fill....exercise! Or what I like to call 'play'*".

Exercise is integral to treating depression, because it produces certain "feel good" hormones that help in the healing process. I am not an exercise enthusiast. But I know if I don't incorporate it in my life, I don't feel as well as I could. I do Zumba some days, water aerobics another; sometimes it's a walk in the neighborhood and sometimes its stretching on the floor in my living room. I must do something.

Playing also means doing things that bring joy. Maybe it's singing in the car, dancing to music in your living room, sitting out in the sun or playing with your dog; yoga or swimming. I know in the midst of your pain it is hard to even conceive of doing these things, but slowly and surely doing them will help. Start by deep breathing and being fully aware of your body.

And one additional "P"!

PREPARATION:

One of the best ways to prevent feeling overwhelmed is to be prepared, in all scenarios. Be organized. Use your calendar. I am not that organized a person, but I try hard. It minimizes the possibility of being overwhelmed. You should see my calendar on my phone! I write everything down- from when I go to exercise, to when I write, to when I pray. I have to, for my own well-being and sanity.

Be prepared when tackling your daily activities. Write down lists and check goals off. Be prepared when encountering difficult emotional situations. Know when you will feel vulnerable and prepare for it. If you know having a difficult conversation with a boss or loved one, for example, is coming up, do what you can to alleviate the pressure. I find writing out my thoughts helps. Be prepared to handle your eating habits, especially if you're an emotional eater like me. Know when to put down the whole bag of cookies and just take two! Your diet, your eating program may also affect the way you feel. Having a healthier, balanced approach to food makes a difference.

Prefer the 'traditional' or 'alternative' approach? Titles aside, the point is treatment is available. You choose! You know what makes you feel comfortable. You don't have to do this on your own. Help, hope and healing are in reach.

Most people diagnosed with mental illness can experience relief from their symptoms by actively participating in an individual treatment plan. Numerous treatments and services for mental illnesses are available. The choice and combination of treatment and services selected depends in most cases on the type of mental illness, the severity of symptoms, the availability of options and decisions determined by the individual, often in consultation with their health care provider and others. Most people with mental illness report that a combination of treatments, services and supports works best to support their recovery. (NAMI)

When I weaned off of my medication my psychiatrist said that it was absolutely necessary that as I go forward I must do two things: exercise and laugh. I use many other forms of self-care but I know without a doubt, these two are absolutely crucial for me. Laughter to me is a miracle and I can't believe I can laugh again!

CHAPTER 7

Suicide is Real But NOT the Answer

In the darkest days of having a mental illness, death may seem like the only way out. I know. I was there. But HELP, HOPE and HEALING are always possible! There is light at the end of the tunnel and laughter will wipe away the tears. Forgive yourself. Forgive others. Love yourself. Love others. You are valuable.

You deserve life. No matter what.

For you formed my inward parts; you knitted me together in my mother's womb. I praise you, for I am fearfully and wonderfully made.

Psalm 139

I WISH I KNEW…

That having suicidal thoughts was a sure fire symptom of depression and that I needed to get help right away.

I was there. I wanted to end my life. In some twisted way, I believed my family would be better off without me. It felt selfless. But it wasn't.

I imagine that Jesus felt suicidal when he knew of his impending destiny in the garden of Gethsemane and he said, "Take this cup from me!" But he did not give in to those thoughts. He gave it over to God, "Thy will be done" and he acted courageously and lived out his purpose.

Courage is something we all have, even if we don't know it. It's inside of us. And we only need to access it. God already put it there when God breathed his Spirit into us in our creation. It is courageous to own our stories of pain. It is courageous to get help. It is courageous to dare to heal. It is courageous to turn away from the darkness. It is courageous to love ourselves. It is courageous to love others. It is courageous to forgive ourselves. It is courageous to forgive others. Being courageous can change your life. Being courageous can save your life. Be courageous. Suicide is not the answer. In fact, it is not an option. You deserve life, no matter what. You are loved. YOU are enough!

SOME FACTS ON SUICIDE:

- Suicide is the 10th leading cause of death in the U.S. (more common than homicide)

- Suicide results in an estimated 1 million deaths globally each year.

- Second only to heart disease, depression is the top reason for suicide in the United States.

- In the US, men are about 4 times more likely to commit suicide than women.

- Among youth aged 15 to 24 suicide is the third leading cause of death.

- More than 90 percent of those who die by suicide had one or more mental disorder.

- One African-American dies by suicide every 4 and 1/2 hours and suicide attempts of African-American males exceed both Caucasian males and females in the U.S.

- The suicide rate for Asian-Americans (6.10 per 10,000) is about half that of the national rate (11.5 per 10,000)

- Among elderly women of all ethnic and racial groups, Asians have the highest suicide rate.

- American Indian /Alaskan Native women aged 15-24 have the highest suicide rate compared to all racial/ethnic groups. The second are for Asian American women.

- Across a recent 15 year span, suicide rates increased 233% among African Americans aged 10-14 compared to 120% among Caucasian Americans in the same age group across the same span of time.

- Each day, about 18 veterans die from suicide.

Adapted from public information from The World Health Organization (WHO, www.who.int), the National Alliance on Mental Illness (NAMI, www.nami.org), Refugee Health Technical Assistance Center (www.refugeehealthta.org) and the National Institute of Mental Health (NIMH, www.nimh.nih.gov).

CHAPTER 8

Healing Takes Time! (Relapse is Possible, NOT Permanent)

When I first started taking medication for my depression I totally expected there to be an immediate, dramatic transformation! I was sorely disappointed to find out that an adequate trial period for a medication, for a response or return to functioning, was approximately 4-6 weeks!!

Be Patient. Don't Give Up

We also glory in our sufferings, because we know that suffering produces perseverance; perseverance, character; and character, hope. And hope does not put us to shame.

Romans 5

I WISH I KNEW...

I wish I knew that healing would not happen overnight, like as soon as I started taking medication! And I wish I knew that relapse could happen and that it is fairly normal to have a setback and then get back on track.

I learned that healing takes time. It is not immediate. It requires persistence, patience and perseverance. Not only may prescription medicine take a period of time to work, approximately 4-6 weeks, in your body and brain, but effective psychotherapy and making lifestyle and behavioral changes which positively affect your mental health condition and lead you on a path to healing, takes time to embrace and implement.

Also, some medications have side effects that may stop you from continuing with the treatment. I remember not being able to stay awake to help my children do their homework. I was so knocked out by the medication. I also gained about 20 pounds on another. Having side effects can certainly dissuade you from going forward. They might want you to stop taking medication altogether! Be patient! Work with your psychiatrist or physician to find the right combination of meds and other forms of treatment. Don't give up!

Two additional things I also came to understand about the journey to healing. One, when you begin to feel better, don't get complacent and stop taking medication, or actively getting help, or doing the things that contribute to your overall recovery. Healing takes time! I stopped taking meds, soon after I began to feel better. I thought, "That's it!" I'm better. But I wasn't. Not yet. I had more work to be done. Even now, I still am committed to my recovery and must be diligent in maintain self-care.

Two, relapse can happen even when you've much improved. So after a period of feeling so much better, after the tears stopped flowing and the energy returned to my body and laughter returned to my soul, something unexpected happened. I had a relapse. I had only known of that word in the context of alcoholism, you know "falling off the wagon", but I never knew that could be true for mental illnesses as well.

It is not unfathomable to have multiple bouts of depressive episodes. In some cases, battling depression is life-long, with periods of wellness and "not wellness." I must remain committed to my healing. I don't ever think I am able to stop being aware of the possibility of relapse.

Knowing that I may relapse acts as a reminder about what could happen if I begin to make different choices. The potential for relapse for me is real and exists every day, nearly every moment of the day. I must be fully aware of the choices I make every day regarding my health. I could find myself heading down that emotional spiral if I am not careful.

I have a Recovery Checklist in my head; perhaps you'll discover your own. I know my triggers; I know what I need to be doing to take care of my health. Am I taking my meds? Am I exercising as I should? Do I really need to eat the whole bag of cookies or just two (individual cookies that is!)? Am I thinking positive thoughts? Am I doing too much? What can I say "no" to?

Relapse may indeed occur, but it is not the end. It is an opportunity: an opportunity to learn and heal some more. Don't worry. It is only temporary.

According to the article "Top Relapse Triggers for Depression & How to Prevent Them" by Margarita Tartakovsky M.S. (www.psychcentral.com) "the risk of recurrence — "relapse after full remission" — for a person who's had one episode of depression is 50 percent. For a person with two episodes, the risk is about 70 percent. For someone with three episodes or more, the risk rises to around 90 percent."

SOME RELAPSE TRIGGERS:

- Interpersonal friction

- Feeling overwhelmed or having too much to do.

- Being judged or criticized

- Ending a relationship

- Physical illness

- Not following treatment

- Ruminating

- Not knowing your personal vulnerabilities

Adapted from public information from The World Health Organization (WHO, www.who.int), the National Alliance on Mental Illness (NAMI, www.nami.org), Refugee Health Technical Assistance Center (www.refugeehealthta.org) and the National Institute of Mental Health (NIMH, www.nimh.nih.gov).

CHAPTER 9

Depression Impacts Those Who Love You, Too

Depression can be debilitating for both you and the people who love and care about you. In the midst of the pain, it may be difficult to empathize with what others may be going through because of your illness. But they are being deeply affected too.

Depression impacts others.

God comforts us in all our troubles, so that we can comfort those in any trouble with the comfort we ourselves receive from God.

2 Corinthians 1

I WISH I KNEW...

I wish I knew that my behavior, born out of my pain, was affecting others like my children and husband and family members. I wish I knew that my illness was not only causing me pain and difficulty but others too.

For much of the initial stages of my depression I did not know what was going on. I literally did not know why I was feeling what I was feeling or why I was behaving the way I was. So many of my conversations with my loved ones would be thwarted when I would respond to pretty straightforward questions like "What's the matter?" or "Why are you sad?" with "I don't know." Not understanding depression and then denying depression prolonged this unproductive and uninformed period and caused much frustration and resentment for all involved.

I thought others could help me by changing their behaviors. I was wrong. My healing had to come from inside me, with appropriate treatment. My loved ones so desperately wanted to help and tried all sorts of approaches, but to no avail. Healing in depression ultimately has to come from within the individual battling depression. According to the book *What to Do When Someone You Love is Depressed* (Golant and Golant, 1996) "…There is a limit to how much you can help (someone you love who is depressed). A person who is depressed must take control of the illness in order to begin to heal. There is a fine line between being helpful and being an enabler-someone who prevents the depressed person from solving his problems himself, thereby allowing them to go untreated."[1]

One thing I learned that has truly stuck with me: when someone you love is depressed, you must take care of yourself and resist wanting to *fix* your spouse, child, parent, friend. You are at risk of depleting yourself and even at risk at becoming depressed yourself. You must take care of yourself. Become a 'strengthened ally'... "having the ability to enjoy simple pleasures in the face of uncertainty...at other times sharing your fears and struggles with someone you trust. It can also mean letting go the reins and having faith in your loved one's ability to cope."[2]

---

[1] What to do When Someone You Love is Depressed (Golant and Golant, 1996) 17.

[2] What to do When Someone You Love is Depressed (Golant and Golant, 1996) 79.

Books like this, Mitch and Susan Golant's "What to Do When Someone You Love is Depressed" shine a light on the potentially severe impact loving and caring for someone with depression can have. "The depression of someone you love can influence your work life and financial status, your emotions, your relationship with your loved one, and your sense of control over your life. It can make you feel stigmatized and alone and can raise your anxiety level."[3] Yet this book and surely others like this, provide helpful techniques and coping strategies for healing in these relationships. "There are things you can do and say, attitudes that you can hold, boundaries and limits that you can establish...[and] there are ways of comforting and taking care of yourself in the

---

[3] What to do When Someone You Love is Depressed (Golant and Golant, 1996) 46.

process…when someone you love is depressed, you need not feel despair. There is hope."[4]

The purpose of this section is to highlight the far-reaching effects of depression. You (the person struggling with depression) may not be able to see it in the midst of the turmoil of depression but your relationships can be deeply affected by the depression. The good news is, relationships can develop "new norms" to cope with the depression and to comfort both the person battling depression and others who love and care for that person.

What is important to remember in this however is that hope abounds! Help is available for both parties. With education about depression, getting effective treatment, support, and love, exercising coping strategies, patience,

---

[4] What to do When Someone You Love is Depressed (Golant and Golant, 1996) 17.

forgiveness, kindness, self-care, becoming a strengthened ally—hope always remains!

SOME FEELINGS YOU MAY EXPERIENCE IF YOU LOVE SOMEONE WHO IS DEPRESSED:

- Lost, afraid, confused.

- You long for the person who was.

- You don't recognize who he or she has become.

- You feel shut out.

- You feel angry and frustrated.

- You feel drained.

- You are desperate for a way to connect.

- You feel guilty and alone.

- You will do anything to help.

SOME ACTIONS YOU CAN TAKE TO ADDRESS THESE FEELINGS:

- Get support yourself.

- Educate yourself.

- Keep a journal.

- Maintain friendships.

- Preserve routines.

- Continue with hobbies.

- Remember that life goes on.

- Learn to let go.

- Gain some perspective.

- Seek respite

- Be mindful of your physical health.

- Deal with your frustration.

- Self-care and setting limits.

Adapted from Golant, Mitch and Golant, Susan, <u>What To Do When Someone You Love is Depressed</u> (Henry Holt and Company, 1996).

CHAPTER 10

There is Always Hope!

This is the most powerful thing I learned about having depression. Especially when the days were so dark and hopeless. Treatment works. Yes, it is a journey and requires all of you- your strength, your energy, your faith, your willingness to get better, your consciousness. Healing IS possible!

There is ALWAYS hope for healing!

Therefore, if anyone is in Christ, [they] are a new creation; old things have passed away; behold, all things have become new!
2 Corinthians 5:17

I WISH I KNEW...

There was light at the end of the tunnel. That healing was possible. That I could one day, experience the miracle of laughter and joy again.

People who experience depression are able to live full, abundant, joyful and productive lives! Raise beautiful families. Love spouses. Maintain healthy relationships. Hold positions of authority and influence. Be creative. Function at high levels. Contribute significantly to all parts of society.

Joy, Life and Light are always within reach! No one promises an easy road towards healing. Instead of a journey of recovery I see it as a journey of discovery. Discover yourself

again! Discover new ways of being! Discover
new possibilities!

THANKS BE TO GOD!